We Will Build a Temple

We Will Build a Temple

The Path of the People of Israel from
King Solomon to John the Baptist

told by

Jakob Streit

Translated by Donald Samson

Illustrated by Susanne Aléthea Mitchell

Printed with support from the Waldorf Curriculum Fund

Published by:
Waldorf Publications at the
Research Institute for Waldorf Education
38 Main Street
Chatham, NY 12037

Title: *We Will Build a Temple*
Author: Jakob Streit
Translator: Donald Samson
Editor: David Mitchell
Proofreaders: Colleen Shetland, Ann Erwin
Illustrations: Susanne A. Mitchell
Cover Art: Susanne A. Mitchell
Cover design: Hallie Wootan

© 2004, 2012 AWSNA Publications
ISBN 1-978-888365-55-9
Reprinted 2017 © Waldorf Publications

First published by Freies Geistesleben with the title:
Lasst uns den Tempel bauen
Original ISBN 3-7725-01072-8

Contents

Foreword	7
Introduction	8
Solomon Becomes King	9
Solomon's Sacrifice and Prayer	9
The Judgment of Solomon	10
Solomon's Wealth and Glory	12
Building the Temple	13
The Division of the Kingdom	15
The Prophet Elijah	17
On Mount Carmel	20
Elijah on Horeb	22
Tobias	25
With Raguel and Sarah	28
Isaiah	31
The Prophecy	33
The Prophet Jeremiah	34
Jeremiah Is Thrown into the Cistern	36
How Jeremiah Saved the Ark of the Covenant	37
The Babylonians Destroy the Temple	39

Daniel	43
Nebuchadnezzar's Dream	45
The Three Men in the Fiery Oven	47
Belshazzar's Feast	48
From Bel to Babel	51
Daniel in the Lion's Den	53
Daniel's Prophecy	56
Nehemiah	57
A Difficult Rebuilding	59
Jonah	61
Heliodorus	66
Job	69
The Test	70
Judas Maccabeus	75
The Alliance with Rome	78
John the Baptist	80
The Strange Encounter	81
John with the Essenes	83
On the Dead Sea	84
The Preacher in the Desert	85
The Baptism of Jesus	87
Concerning the Death of the Baptist	89

Foreword

The Biblical stories retold in this book by Jakob Streit are based on the Old Testament. They connect us intensely with the pictures and events that contributed to the forming of Western culture at its beginning.

The pictures provided are not sentimental and certainly do not represent present consciousness. Some of the stories may be considered violent, sexist, and even racist. Before sharing these stories with the children, the parent or teacher would benefit by calling forth within themselves the historical/religious context of these events. We must expect that the children will have many questions requiring carefully thought-through answers.

An experience which surprised me was that, as I contemplated the stories at a level beneath the surface, I developed a deeper understanding of many contemporary problems in the Middle East.

– David Mitchell

Introduction

The present volume is the conclusion of a trilogy of stories from the Old Testament. The previous volumes were *And There Was Light* (From Creation to Noah's Ark) and *Journey to the Promised Land* (The Path of the People of Israel from Abraham's Calling to David's Dream).

Aside from the books of the Old Testament, apocryphal writings were used, in particular the five volumes *Tales of the Jews* by Micha Joseph Bin Gorion. They provide rich pictures and a colorful depiction of the stories, while being thoroughly true to the sources.

May these stories of kings and prophets, whose destinies shed light upon the wait for the coming Messiah, make the world of the Old Testament more available to children.

– Jakob Streit

Solomon Becomes King

When King David had grown very old, he sent a message to the prophet Nathan and to the Priest Zadok: "Anoint my son Solomon as king. Announce it to all the people with trumpet blast! Let him ride upon a mule, and lead him into my palace! Walk with him to the throne!" They carried out David's wishes as he asked.

During his time as king, David had amassed great treasures of gold, silver and precious stones. He spoke to his son Solomon: "I give all of this treasure over to you for the building of the temple." So David's great treasure was passed on to Solomon for the purpose of building a praiseworthy temple in Jerusalem.

When King David died, the Lord filled Solomon's spirit with wisdom so that he could rule the people with righteousness and build the temple as a holy sanctuary.

Solomon's Sacrifice and Prayer

King Solomon once went to Gibeon in order to take a burnt offering on the top of the mountain. In the night, the voice of God spoke to him thus: "Solomon, you may ask of Me a boon. What gift should I give to you?"

Solomon responded: "Lord, give to me a wise and judicious heart with which to rule the people; a heart that can tell the good from the evil."

The voice of God answered: "You shall have a thoughtful and wise heart. It will bring you both honor and riches."

Solomon awoke and realized it had been but a dream; but this was a dream that had spoken the truth.

The Judgment of Solomon

A servant stepped before Solomon's throne one day and spoke, "Two women stand before the door. They request a hearing."

Solomon answered, "Tell them in my name they are welcome."

When the two women entered, they fell to their knees before the throne. One of them had a child in her arms; the other carried only a blanket. The king spoke to the childless woman. "Speak of your complaint; what do you wish? If you are in the right, your wish will be fulfilled!"

The woman answered with great emotion, "This woman's house and mine are next to each other. Yester eve, I lay down to sleep with my child. When I woke up early this morning, I found her dead child in my chamber. My own child had disappeared!"

With a sharp tongue the second woman cried out, "That's not true; you lie! You deceive the king! Your child is dead, mine is alive. O King, pass judgment! Give me satisfaction!" In this way, the two women contended for the child who was still alive.

Solomon spoke to his servant, "Take your sword. Divide the child in half! Give to each of the women one of the halves."

The woman to his left said, "Yes, yes, the child should be divided between us! One half for me, the other half for you. I will be content with that!" With these words, she held the child out to the servant.

In the heart of the real mother, however, a true love for her child flared up. She cried out, "Ah, King, no! Do not divide it! Spare that tender life! I'd rather give her the child, even though she lies."

Solomon replied, "Stay your hand, arms-bearer! Do not cut the child in half! The woman who says she would rather give away the child than see it dead, she is the true mother."

When the servant placed the little one into her arms, tears fell onto the child's face. The thankful mother stretched her arms toward Solomon, and he made the sign of a blessing over the child.

The other woman jumped up quickly and tried to flee. The servant, though, held her fast by the arm. She sank down before Solomon's throne and begged, "Forgive me, King, for this sin that I have committed! The pain over the death of my own child confused my senses."

When Solomon saw her remorse and her suffering, he said, "Stand up! Go from here and sin no more!"

It did not take long before the whole city of Jerusalem was talking about the two women and the child who was, in the end, not cut in half. Praise for Solomon's wisdom and fairness spread throughout the land.

Solomon's Wealth and Glory

Solomon built many cities and his wealth increased. His ships sailed over the seas and brought abundant trade merchandise into his land. The king of Tyre sent to him cedars from Lebanon and many carpenters. Solomon had them build for him a magnificent palace.

Next he wanted the resourceful carpenters to construct a temple as a House of God in Jerusalem. His father, King David, had left him this undertaking when he died. The temple was to be similar to the holy tent, the Tabernacle, which stood on the heights of Gibeon. Since the time of Moses, that had been the only House of God in which the priests carried out their offices. It had now grown old and was to be replaced by the new temple in the middle of Jerusalem. It was planned to be twice as large, built strongly of wood and stone, just as God had revealed it should be to Moses on Mount Sinai. The holy chest, the Ark of the Covenant, which held the tablets containing the Ten Commandments Moses had brought down from Sinai, would again be set up in the Holy of Holies.

Building the Temple

Solomon hired thousands of able Phoenician carpenters; a great host of workers from Israel joined them. He asked Hiram from Tyre, famous for his master work with bronze, to direct the construction. Hiram accepted the commission. He understood how to melt and pour metals. He crafted two mighty pillars out of bronze, Jachin and Boaz, which were set up to be the "watchmen" before the temple doors. The temple itself had an entrance hall, and then came the sanctuary which only the priests were allowed to enter. A five-cornered door led into the furthest room, the Holy of Holies. After its consecration, not even the priests were allowed to enter this last room. It was dedicated alone to the spirit of God and the Ark of the Covenant. All of the interior walls of the temple were inset with plates of gold.

When the construction of the building was finished, there was a great festival for the dedication. The Ark of the Covenant and all of the implements were brought from the Tabernacle and made ready in front of the temple. Only when the wood for the sacrificial fire had been prepared on the great altar in front of the temple could priests carry the implements within. The trumpets blared and the High Priest called out,

> *Carry hither to the consecrated place*
> *the holy chest of the Commandments!*

Supported by long carrying poles, twelve priests brought the Ark of the Covenant into the Holy of Holies. The trumpets sounded once again, and the High Priest called out,

> *Carry within the golden Seraph angels,*
> *place them beside the holy chest,*
> *to the right and to the left,*
> *so that the tips of their wings are touching!*

When all of this was done, the High Priest closed the doors to the Holy of Holies. He withdrew into the long temple hall, which was called the sanctuary. Each time, before he called out, the trumpets resounded. Once again, he cried out loudly,

> *Bring in the candelabrum!*
> *Seven times branch its arms,*
> *in accordance with the number of planets.*

Ten priests—there were ten, one for each of the commandments—carried the candelabrum into the temple hall. When this was done, the High Priest cried out,

> *Arrange now the loaves by twelve*
> *as a celestial ring in the House of the Lord!*

Solemnly the priests placed the loaves on the golden table as a symbol for the expansive world of the stars. The trumpets resounded, and the High Priest called out again,

> *Hang before the door to the Holy of Holies*
> *the curtain in the colors of the four elements!*

Lastly, the altar for holding the incense vessels was carried within, and soon a wondrous scent spread throughout the temple.

When all of this was completed, Solomon and the priests walked into the inner courtyard and stood before the high altar. All of the forecourts of the temple were filled with people. Trumpets played a song of praise. The life of the city gave itself over to silence and devotion.

Solomon threw himself down before the altar and prayed to the Lord for His blessings. The priests and the collected folk followed his example. When the last 'amen' was spoken, a bolt of lightning shot out of heaven and struck the pile of wood on the altar and ignited the sacrificial fire. A peal of thunder shook the people. All eyes looked up to the heavens. A cloud sank down from above and settled, glowing over the temple. At this the people whispered to one another, "Now the glory of the Lord fills the temple and sanctifies it."

Solomon announced loudly, "From this point on, only the priests may enter the inner rooms of the temple! The fire on the altar, ignited from the heavens, shall burn continuously, day and night, so long as the temple stands!" From among their number, the priests assigned guardians of the fire, so that it would never go out.

When the sacrifice was concluded, Solomon stepped up to the immense water basin that was supported by twelve bronze bulls. Master Hiram had cast it and it was called "the bronze sea." Every bull was so cleverly created that water flowed out from its mouth. This provided the priests with water to purify themselves before performing a sacrifice.

Following the celebration, the Israelites said among themselves, "Jerusalem and our people have been given a heart!" The fire on the altar before the temple burned from that day on, both day and night, through the centuries.

The Division of the Kingdom

When a good, noble deed has brought blessings to people, Satan rises up in order to mix it with evil. This happened to Solomon as well. As he grew older and his spirit grew weaker, evil repeatedly stole upon him in the night. The king allowed altars to be erected on three hills to bear foreign idols so that visitors coming into his kingdom from other lands could also worship. Solomon even repeatedly took part in their sacrifices. In this manner he went astray, and the light of the temple paled.

Following Solomon's death, a conflict arose in the kingdom. Solomon's son Rehoboam was rather haughty. Only two tribes remained true to him, Judah and Benjamin, together with the capital Jerusalem. The other ten tribes formed a northern kingdom, and chose as their king Jeroboam, who had been Solomon's capable servant. They called their realm Israel, and Jeroboam made his residence in the city of Shechem. In order that his people would also have a sanctuary and not need to make the pilgrimage to Jerusalem, Jeroboam built at once two sanctuaries with calves of gold. His people prayed at the altars of these Egyptian idols.

Troubles and skirmishes broke out repeatedly between these two sibling realms, and great misery descended upon the land of Palestine. When the particularly wicked King Ahab ruled Israel, God awoke the prophet Elijah. He came as a true man of God to confront the depravity of the people and the royal house.

The Prophet Elijah

Ahab, the king of Israel, married Jezebel, a princess from the distant realm of Sidonia. She was a haughty woman and it was rumored that she was a sorceress. Jezebel brought with her in a wagon not only her own graven images but also priests of her god Baal. Ahab, the king, was compelled to build for her god a temple in the royal city of Samaria. This false temple became a rival to Solomon's sanctuary in Jerusalem. The people of Israel quickly abandoned their worship of the God of Abraham, Isaac and Jacob.

A terrible drought fell over the land. No rain fell, and in the night there was no dew. At first the grasses died, then the plants and the trees. Then the animals died, and the fields dried up and turned into a desert. In the dreadful famine that followed, people began to die.

At this time, near the city of Samaria, lived Naboth, a farmer. Through him spoke the lofty spirit of a messenger of God, Elijah. God spoke to him thus: "Go among the folk and speak with them so that they abandon praying to false idols. Do this in secret and without revealing who you are."

Elijah appeared in huts, in villages and along solitary paths. He urged the people to serve the one God. His words were so urgent that their hearts were moved, and they obeyed. Whenever they wanted to invite the mysterious prophet to stay longer or give him a place to stay for the night, he was gone. Soon he would appear in another place and move the souls of the people there. Everywhere they spoke of the hidden prophet and no one knew who he was.

News of this new prophet also reached King Ahab and Jezebel. The whole story seemed uncanny to them. The king suspected that some plot against him was stirring. Jezebel wondered, "How can we keep this prophet from doing us harm?"

The king sent spies out to track down this unknown menace, but no one was able to find him. The voice of God, however, spoke to Elijah: "Go to King Ahab and tell him the people must restore their trust in the God of Abraham. Until they do this, no rain will fall on the land."

So unexpectedly one day the prophet stood at the portal of the king's palace. He said to the guard, "Tell the king that the prophet is here and wishes to speak with him."

When the king heard this, he grew frightened; still, he had the prophet brought before him. With forceful words Elijah announced to the king, "No rain will fall upon the land until you and your people return again to the true God!" After speaking these words he left the palace and disappeared.

God spoke to Naboth-Elijah: "Go into the solitude of the Cherith Wadi. Strengthen your heart there to appear before the king and the people." In the stillness of a cave Elijah gave himself over to deep prayer and received strengthening light from the spiritual world.

There was still a little water flowing in the Cherith Wadi from which Elijah could drink. Every day two ravens appeared and brought him something to eat so that he could stay alive while in hiding. But then the brook dried up, and the voice of God directed Elijah to go to Zarephath. As Elijah came to the gates of the city, he encountered a widow who was gathering wood. He sat down nearby on a stone. The woman looked at him and saw that the stranger was dying of thirst. He spoke to her. "Can you bring me some water and bread? I'm parched."

She answered, "I have no bread, only a little leftover flour and oil. It won't be long before my son and I also die of hunger."

She fetched a water jug and gave the stranger something to drink. He then said to her, "Make with your flour and oil a flatbread. You will not run out of flour and oil."

She went and did what the stranger had told her to do, and she did not run out of flour and oil. Every day after that Elijah, the widow, and her son had enough to eat. Elijah stayed with them on the top floor in their house.

A little while after this, the boy grew so ill there was no sign of life left in him. Elijah picked him up and carried him to his upstairs chamber and laid him down on his own bed. Three times he bent over the boy and cried out, "Oh, Lord, my God, let this child's life return to his body!'"

Behold! Life once again stirred in the boy. Elijah carried him down to his mother and said, "Woman, behold, your son is alive!"

Full of awe she said, "Now I know that you are a man of God and a true prophet!"

On Mount Carmel

When the misery in the land was at its greatest, the voice of God spoke to Elijah: "Go and appear before King Ahab! By means of a sacrifice on Mount Carmel, you will bring rain to the land."

Elijah came before the king, and Ahab cried out to him, "Is that you, the cause of Israel's woes?"

Elijah answered, "It is not I who brings woes upon Israel, but rather you and your house. You have forsaken the God of your fathers and you have seduced the people into the idol worship of Baal. Listen to me, O King: Gather your people on Mount Carmel together with all of the priests who serve Baal. Have the priests erect a pile of wood for a sacrificial fire, but they are not to ignite it.

I will do the same. Then the priests of Baal will call upon their god to send fire. I will then call upon the God of our fathers. The God who ignites the sacrificial fire from heaven, He is the true God."

Ahab sent messengers throughout all of Israel and ordered the people and the priests to gather on Mount Carmel. On the designated day, two sacrificial altars were built and two sacrificial animals were placed beside them. The priests of Baal built an immense altar. They strode about wearing colorful clothing and decorated high hats. Elijah, wearing a plain gown, had twelve stones piled on top of one another, one stone for each of the tribes of the people.

Elijah lifted his voice and spoke to the assembled people. "Only I am left as prophet of the Lord. The prophets of Baal number four hundred and fifty! Let them call upon their Baal. Let him ignite their sacrifice. Afterwards, I will call upon the name of the Lord. The God who answers with fire is the true God."

Immediately, the priests of Baal began to dance wildly about their altar and cried continuously, "Baal, hear us, send us fire! Baal, hear us, send us fire!"

It is told that the priests of Baal had secretly hidden one of their own under the pile of wood with a pan holding ashes and glowing coals. He was supposed to blow on them and secretly kindle the fire when they called upon Baal. A poisonous snake, however, had slithered underneath the pile of wood. It bit the hidden priest in the leg; even before his fellow priests had begun to cry out, he lay there dead.

The dancing priests cried out ever louder and louder to Baal, but no sign of fire showed itself. They began to rave and started to stab themselves in their own flesh with knives and swords so that as they danced the blood ran down and splashed on the ground. Still no fire appeared.

Elijah lifted his powerful voice and cried out to all the people, "Gather around me!"

He had the bull sacrificed according to ancient custom, laid upon the pile of wood and then had consecrated water poured over it. Then he prayed to God, "O Lord, hear me! Let your people know that you are the true God!"

There was a flash of lightning from heaven, and it set fire to the sacrifice. The people cried out in fear and joy, "The Lord is our God! The Lord alone is our God!"

In this way the prophecy was fulfilled and the priests of Baal overthrown. Elijah climbed up to the top of Mount Carmel. He bowed down upon the earth and put his face between his knees. Then he looked toward the distant sea. Over the water a small cloud began to form, and he watched as it grew to be a great cloud. Storm-winds began to roar. An enormous downpour drenched the land. The brooks and streams began once again to flow. The wells filled up and after several days fresh grass sprang up out of the dried earth.

Elijah on Horeb

King Ahab told his wife Jezebel everything that Elijah had done on the mountain. Jezebel, however, was a fanatic follower in the service of Baal and made every effort to have Elijah murdered. Elijah learned of this dark intention. He fled into the desert and left his servant in Beer-sheba. That evening, before he laid himself to sleep beneath a broom bush, he prayed, "Lord, take my life! I've had enough."

In the night, however, an angel of the Lord touched him and said, "Arise and eat! You still have a long way to go."

He found in that place food and drink and wandered from there day by day to Mount Horeb in Sinai, where he withdrew into a cave. At this place he received divine revelation so that his soul became ever more like that of the angels. For forty days he immersed himself in this solitude, just as Moses had once experienced here.

As Elijah returned, he met a farmer out in the fields, plowing the earth with his oxen. Elijah stepped up to him and asked, "What is your name?"

The ploughman answered, "Elisha!"

Then Elijah recognized this man as his disciple and successor. He cast his mantle upon him as a sign that he had taken him under his protection.

The ploughman said, "I will follow you! Let me only go to kiss my father and mother, and then I will go with you."

In this way, Elisha became the disciple of the prophet Elijah. For the remaining time that Elijah was given to walk the earth, his faithful student Elisha never strayed from his side.

The great prophet knew the time when he would have to depart from the earth. He went with Elisha and several disciples to the river Jordan. Elijah rolled his mantle up and struck the water with it. The waters of the river parted to either side. Only Elisha, however, was allowed to walk over to the other side with the prophet. When the two arrived at the other shore, Elijah said, "Ask what I should do for you, before I am taken from you."

Elisha said, "May your spirit be with me in all the difficult times."

As they spoke, a flaming wagon led by fiery-winged horses descended to them. Elijah mounted it and flew toward heaven. He let go of his mantle, however, and it fell right at Elisha's feet. Elisha picked it up and walked upon the shores of the Jordan. Then he took the mantle and struck the water with it, just as Elijah had done. The waters parted and made an open path. Now Elisha knew for certain that the power and strength of the prophet was with him. The disciples of the prophet were waiting for him on the other shore. When they saw Elisha striding through the Jordan, they bowed in reverence and said, "The spirit of Elijah rests upon Elisha!"

Elisha performed many miracles: He made foul water pure; he healed the ill and those with leprosy; he made more food out of less; and he even brought a dead boy back to life again. For the people he was a bringer of peace; he could even, through reconciliation and compromise, prevent war.

Elisha anointed the able commander of the army, Jehu, to be a king to stand against Ahab and Jezebel. Jehu wiped out the services to Baal and destroyed the temple to Baal. He became the punishing judge for Ahab, Jezebel and their house: He brought their rule, which had caused so much harm to the land and the people, to an end.

Tobias

One of the few Jewish people who had not turned to worshiping idols was Tobias. He was also among those captured Israelites who had been dragged off to the land of the Assyrians. However, through his competence in service to the king, he had earned great respect. He owned a house and had material goods. But many of his Israelite brethren were held as slaves and lived in misery.

Tobias and Hanna, his wife, had only one son whose name was also Tobias. He was called Tobias the Younger. The father often took the young Tobias with him when he had business to attend. Occasionally, they came to places where Israelites lived in poverty and were forced into hard labor. Tobias the Elder comforted the people, gave them advice in dealing with illnesses and taught them the Hebrew prayers. Tobias the Younger would have a basket or sack with him and was always allowed to give something to the poor and the hungry. In this way, father Tobias softened a great deal of misery and a good heart blossomed in the boy.

At this time, King Shalmaneser died. His son, Sennacherib, pressed the Israelites even harder than before. Some would even be beaten to death over a little thing. When the new king learned that Tobias the Elder was going among the Israelites bringing aid, he became irate. He took away Tobias' house and possessions, and Tobias was forced to flee with Hanna and their son.

After forty-five days of kingship, the terrible King Sennacherib was slain by his own sons. Tobias was allowed to return to his own house and all of his possessions were returned to him.

One day, father Tobias was resting in the sun along the wall of his house. Droppings from a swallow's nest hugging the wall above him fell, landing right in Tobias' eyes. This resulted in his going blind. He now felt his life so shadowed by this that he thought God was soon going to collect his soul to Him. He summoned his son and spoke to him, "Here in this chamber, under the roof, runs a thick wooden beam. Around in the middle, a piece of parchment is stuck in a crack. Reach it down to me!"

Tobias found the yellowed parchment and placed it in his father's hands. His father continued to speak, "When you were still a child, I lent ten pounds of silver to Gabael who lives in the city of Rages in the land of Medea. He attested to the truth of this with his signature on this piece of parchment. Gabael is an honest man; make the journey to him! He will give back to you the borrowed silver in return for this piece of parchment. Seek out a traveling companion. May the blessings of God rest upon you!"

When the young Tobias had prepared himself for the journey, he embraced both father and mother and then departed. Hardly had he left his home when he encountered a handsome youth who walked with a curiously light step. Tobias could not know that this was an angel who had taken on the appearance of a human being. Tobias' dog was walking beside him, and it sprang joyously forward to greet the unknown man.

Tobias addressed the stranger, "I am looking for a traveling companion. Would you like to come with me? I will not find a better companion than you. Will you come with me into the land of the Medes?"

With a clear voice the youth answered, "I will journey with you there. You can call me Azariah." When the youth offered his hand as a pact for their agreement of traveling together, Tobias felt as if a warming fire rippled through him.

Their first day's journey brought them to the river Tigris. Tobias wanted to bathe his tired feet in the water. A large fish was swimming there and snapped at his toes. Tobias cried out and his companion called to him, "Grab the fish by the fins. Pull it out of the water!"

Tobias did this and landed the fish. He cut the fish up and broiled it for their evening meal.

The youth said, "Don't throw away the bile of the fish, but rather take it with you. Take good care of it!"

Tobias asked, "Tell me, Azariah, what should I do with the bile?"

The youth answered, "It is medicine for the eyes. Take it with you for your father!"

With Raguel and Sarah

When they reached the first city in the land of Medea, Azariah said, "There is a man who lives in this land by the name of Raguel who is a relative of yours. He has only a single daughter whose name is Sarah. If you would ask her father for her hand in marriage, I assure you that it will make you very happy."

Tobias was amazed that Azariah knew all of this, and he agreed to go and visit his relatives. When they arrived, Tobias revealed who he was. Raguel wept tears of joy and said, "You are my brother's son! You are the son of a pious man."

Since Tobias found Raguel's daughter Sarah quite lovely, he decided to remain there until the wedding. He said to the youth Azariah, "Would you be willing to travel to the city of Rages with this piece of parchment? Seek out there the venerable Gabael and give the parchment to him. Invite him to join us here for the wedding."

Azariah hesitated for a moment, glancing up, as if he wanted to read a message in the clouds. Then he smiled and nodded in agreement. After several days he returned with Gabael for the wedding. Gabael said to Tobias, "When I was in great need, your father helped me with a loan of silver. Now I have attained gold and property. Here is the borrowed silver to be returned to your father."

Azariah behaved strangely. He would often disappear for several days in a row. However, when it was time to travel, he was suddenly back again. After a few days, Tobias said, "I know that my parents are very worried about my staying away for so long. Perhaps they fear that death may have found me. Dear Sarah, let us depart from your parents and make the return journey to my own home."

Raguel gave to them gifts and beasts to ride on for their return; Azariah traveled with them. After a long journey, when they approached the entry yard of Tobias' parents, his little dog suddenly ran out and announced the arrival of his master. Then came the young Tobias himself, and he brought with him not only the silver, but also a dear, young wife. Azariah stood off to the side as they greeted one another and left them to their joy. Then, however, he stepped over to young Tobias and spoke softly to him, "Smear your father's eyes with the gall from the fish. He will be able to see once again!"

Straightaway father Tobias lay down, and his son smeared the gall onto his eyes. As the father lay there for a time, a white film was freed and little by little clear light came into his eyes. The father saw Sarah with Tobias, saw Azariah, and thanked heaven for the miracle and all the good that he had experienced.

Suddenly Azariah came nearer and began to speak. "May angels ever and again guide the destiny of human beings! Now you should learn the full truth of my origin: I am Raphael, the healing angel of God!"

Wonder and shock struck the gathering, which until now had been so joyful; fear and trembling took hold of them all. They bowed deeply down to the ground. Azariah's voice spoke, "Give thanks to the Lord! Proclaim His glory!"

When they once again dared to raise their heads, Azariah-Raphael had disappeared. Where he had stood, a shining light was dissolving like a cloud. The old father began to sing a song of praise, and their joy and thankfulness knew no end.

Isaiah

At the time when the captured Israelites were forced to live in exile in the realm of the Assyrians, good King Hezekiah continued to rule in Jerusalem. The prophet of God, Isaiah, was his friend and teacher. Hezekiah knew that the people of Israel living in the north had grown weak because they had served foreign gods and had strayed from the belief of their fathers. For this reason the Assyrian King Shalmaneser had been able to conquer Israel and take thousands into captivity.

King Hezekiah was convinced by the prophet Isaiah that the land of Judah ought to be completely freed from idol worshiping. He ordered the altars of foreign gods torn down wherever they were to be found: on the mountains, in the forests, or at the bases of trees. Isaiah preached ardently to the people of the true belief in the God of their forefathers. This was a difficult task, since many had found pleasure in the pagan customs.

Isaiah said, "When the people of Judah choose the path of righteousness, we need not have any fear of the Assyrians."

Now the Assyrian King Shalmaneser died, and his son Sennacherib became his successor. He looked greedily at Jerusalem and thought to himself, "I could conquer this land with its splendid city, just as my father conquered the northern kingdom of Israel. There are treasures of silver and gold in the temple and in the royal palace of Jerusalem. I will take them and subjugate the land of Judea."

Sennacherib sent to King Hezekiah a threat and demanded he pay in tribute a treasure of gold and silver. King Hezekiah was a man of peace and willingly sent to him a great deal of gold and silver in order to insure the peace. In Sennacherib, however, a greedy dragon had taken hold of his soul. He wanted more! He wanted all the land of King Hezekiah and the city of Jerusalem.

In search of counsel, Hezekiah sent messengers to the prophet Isaiah. Isaiah knew how to deal with every crisis. In his deepest prayers he turned to God. He responded to the king's messengers, "Say to your king: Have no fear of the Assyrians. God will be with us and with Jerusalem." Upon their return, the messengers reported to King Hezekiah what they had learned from Isaiah.

King Sennacherib raised a great army and took to the field against Jerusalem. Hezekiah, sunk in deepest prayer, awaited the approaching enemy. All of the gates of the city were closed. The high walls were strong. With their immense army, the Assyrians besieged the city of Jerusalem with the intention of breaking their opposition with hunger and thirst. In the middle of the night, however, unusual peals of thunder began and grew louder. Horrified, the Assyrian warriors perceived above the besieged city the light of an immense fire that threw out sparks in every direction, reaching right into their own camp.

Terrified, many fled, and before all others ran the horsemen on their wild mounts. Others fell to the ground unconscious and remained lying there as if dead. Sennacherib fled together with his field commanders. The campaign of the Assyrians ended in terror. Shortly thereafter, Sennacherib was slain in his own land.

On the morning after the Assyrian army took flight, Isaiah and King Hezekiah spoke to the delivered people, "Give thanks to the Lord, who has delivered you through the miracle of His might!"

The Prophecy

Once Isaiah tarried in the wilderness. It was deepest night. As he sat deep in prayer, the darkness was lifted from his eyes. In the brightest of light the image of God with the Heavenly Hosts appeared before him. One of the seraphim hovered over him and touched his lips with the glowing fire of the heavens. He received the ability to speak pure, strong words. Isaiah then heard the voice of God, which asked, "Whom shall I send out?"

Isaiah called, "I am ready. Send me!"

The divine word came to Isaiah. Within his spirit he was able to see into distant future times. He foresaw the complete destruction of the temple, and he saw the coming of the Messiah. He announced these events to the people. And these are the words of Isaiah:

"Behold, a virgin will give birth to a son, and his name will be Emmanuel.

"A branch will spring from the root of David, and the Spirit of the Lord will rest upon him.

"God will come and release you. Then the eyes of the blind will be opened; the ears of the deaf will hear again.

"He will slay the tyrant. Righteousness and faithfulness will once again hold sway. Peace will spread and the wolf will sleep by the side of the lambs."

So Isaiah gave to his people the certainty that out of their lineage the Messiah, the Deliverer, would one day be born.

The Prophet Jeremiah

When Jehoiakim was king over Judea, he became friends with the Pharaoh of Egypt. Jehoiakim was interested only in increasing the splendor of his palace by imitating the Egyptians. On many mountaintops and in valleys idol worshiping was once again taking hold.

The prophet Jeremiah came forward against these practices. "You are a blinded people! Why are you serving foreign idols! The Lord of the world is with you, when you serve the true God. Idols are made with an ax from the wood of the forest. They are made beautiful with silver and gold; with hammer and nail they are secured so they do not totter. They are the same as the scarecrows in the field; they are not able to speak. They have to be carried because they cannot move about on their own. But the Lord is a living God! The earth shakes before His wrath. He created it in His wisdom."

There was a place in the Hinnom Valley near Jerusalem where the idol worshiping was especially evil. The altars to Moloch stood in this place. On these altars even small children were sacrificed. The altar stones were splattered with human blood. Once, after such a sacrifice had taken place, Jeremiah approached with several faithful friends. They were carrying a large, clay vessel that the prophet had convinced them to bring along. When they reached the altar to Moloch, Jeremiah climbed up to a spot from which he could be seen and heard. His friends held the clay vessel up in the air in front of him. Full of curiosity, people came and asked, "What's going on here?"

Jeremiah began, "Hear the word of the Lord, dwellers of Jerusalem! Harm will come to you because you defile this place with the blood of innocent children and sacrifice them to the fire. Just as I now break this jug into a thousand fragments, so will Jerusalem be destroyed!" Jeremiah grasped the clay vessel and smashed it on the altar to Moloch. The crowd became terribly agitated, but no one dared to lay a hand on the prophet.

Following this, Jeremiah went to the city of Jerusalem. He entered the courtyard of the temple and repeated the prophecy about the fall of Jerusalem. A chief officer of the temple heard these words and became angry. He ordered Jeremiah to be arrested. Jeremiah was bound and placed in the stocks at one of the city gates and those who passed by ridiculed him.

On the next day, when he was released, Jeremiah withdrew into the wilderness. His friend, Baruch, wrote down in a book the divine prophecy that Jeremiah dictated to him.

Baruch took this parchment and stood before the people in the market places, reading in a loud voice what was written there. A royal servant took the book away and brought it to King Jehoiakim. Since it was winter he was sitting before a pan filled with coals warming himself. The chancellor had to read to him Jeremiah's words. The king, though, was deaf to their message. He ripped the parchment piece by piece into shreds and threw them into the glowing coals.

Not long after this Jehoiakim died an ugly death. His successor, King Zedekiah, also would not hear the warnings of Jeremiah.

Jeremiah Is Thrown into the Cistern

Once again Jeremiah spoke to the people of the danger threatening Jerusalem and said that in the near future it would be destroyed. He foretold, "Whoever remains in this city will die by sword, hunger or illness. Whoever surrenders to the Chaldeans will be spared. The city will come under the rule of the kings of Babylon."

Several nobles then spoke to King Zedekiah, "Someone ought to kill this Jeremiah. He lames both the hands and the courage of the soldiers."

The nobles were very powerful, so Zedekiah answered, "I deliver him into your hands!" They took Jeremiah and lowered him by a rope into a cistern at the guard's quarters near the palace. They expected him to die there. There was no water left inside, only wet slime.

A high-ranking servant of the king had taken note of what they did to Jeremiah. Since he had learned only good things from the prophet, the servant sought out the king and spoke to him. "The nobles have dealt with Jeremiah in an evil manner. He lies beneath the guard's quarters in the slime of a cistern and he will die of hunger. Consider carefully, O king; he is still a man of God!"

Zedekiah ordered, "Take three men with you. Pull the prophet out before he dies. Bring him to me through the secret door. I want to speak with him."

The servant chose his helpers. They lowered a rope into the cistern and told Jeremiah to tie himself onto the end. Once he did this, they were able to pull him up again to the light of day.

After Jeremiah had washed the slime off and been given clean clothes, the servant led him through a hidden passage to King Zedekiah. It was important that the nobles learn nothing of this.

Zedekiah asked Jeremiah, "What is going to happen to Jerusalem? Withhold nothing from me! Tell me the whole truth!"

Jeremiah replied, "When I tell you everything, O king, you will have me killed Even when I give you advice, you will not listen to me anyway."

Then and there, the king swore an oath, "You will not suffer any injury. I will not again place you into the hands of men who want to take your life."

Then Jeremiah began to speak, "It has thus been revealed to me: If you willingly surrender to the king of Babylon, your own life will be spared, and the city will not be burnt. But if you do not surrender, Jerusalem will be destroyed and you will die as well."

King Zedekiah was horrorstruck. He said, "No one may learn about our conversation. If, however, the nobles hear about it and ask you: 'What have you spoken about with the king?' then say: 'I have asked him if I might be allowed to stay in the palace watchtower.'"

Jeremiah agreed to do this. He remained for only a short time in the watchtower. Then the voice of the Lord came to him to remove the Ark of the Covenant from the temple before the arrival of the Chaldeans.

How Jeremiah Saved the Ark of the Covenant

When the Babylonian King Nebuchadnezzar set out to conquer and destroy Jerusalem and pillage the temple, Jeremiah received the divine order to take the Ark of the Covenant with the tablets of the Ten Commandments to a safe place.

Once, from the heights of Mount Nebo, God had let Moses and his tribe behold the land of Canaan at the end of their long wandering through the desert. Afterwards, God had taken Moses to Himself. The earth had opened and received his body. It was not possible to find his remains, so Moses has no grave.

To that very place, to the heights of Mount Nebo, Jeremiah was to bring the Ark of the Covenant. When Jeremiah came with

his friends to the temple, they found that the whole city was in a commotion as a result of the approaching Babylonians. People were bringing food into the city and strengthening the walls and gates. In the midst of this tumult, Jeremiah found that the priests of the temple were in despair over the fate of the sanctuary in the event that Nebuchadnezzar actually managed to break into Jerusalem.

Jeremiah called the priests together. "It is God's will that we bring the Ark with the Ten Commandments out of Jerusalem to a secure place that God has shown me!"

No one tried to stop him and his followers. At night, by the light of torches, he and the priests entered the inner sanctum of the temple. The sanctuary was brightly lit by the ten lamps that burned day and night.

Jeremiah lifted the curtain to the Holy of Holies. The light of the torches reflected a gleam of gold from the walls and from the two cherubim. Four priests lifted the Holy Ark and carried it out. Others took several of the holy vessels and instruments and wrapped them up in cloths. In the light of the torches, they carried what they had saved out through the gates and over the heights of Jerusalem toward the south.

When after a long journey Jeremiah and his following reached Mount Nebo, he indicated to the carriers a cave. They brought the Ark of the Covenant and the instruments inside. Jeremiah had them close up the opening to the cave with stone, sand and earth. No one should find it again, unless led by divine inspiration.

The Babylonians Destroy the Temple

Nebuchadnezzar arrived at Jerusalem with an immense army. The Babylonians surrounded and besieged the city from all sides so that no one was able to leave it. In the fourth month of the siege, when hunger had claimed its first victims, King Zedekiah ordered his soldiers to secretly begin to dismantle the city walls from the inside, so that they could flee through the breach in the night and escape the Babylonians.

The breakout occurred in the dark of night. The king fled with his retainers through the midst of the sleeping enemy. Soon, however, the Babylonians followed him on foot, then hunted him with horses and caught up with him on the plains of Jericho. They dragged him off in triumph to Babylon where soon after, he and his followers met a terrible end.

Through the very breach that King Zedekiah's followers tore open in the city wall for their own flight, the army of the Babylonians was then, in the night, able to enter. Armed with weapons and carrying burning torches, they stormed over the ruins of the wall into the city. A great lamentation arose. Whoever stood in their way was cut down. Here and there the invaders threw their torches into the houses. Soon, even the wooden structure of the king's palace was ablaze. The flames illuminated the gruesome slaughter.

Many young and old Israelite soldiers hastened to the temple in order to defend it. The walls of the temple courtyard offered protection. Desperately, the Israelites fought in the burning city to save their Sanctuary. Young archers climbed up on the high altar in the outer courtyard. The Babylonians, however, had brought ladders, and they were able to scale the courtyard walls. In the glow of the flames, and often blinded by the dense smoke, it was difficult to tell friend from foe.

The Babylonians were set on stealing the gold and other treasures from the temple. They were under orders not to set any fires in the temple until everything had been plundered. When they climbed over the last inner wall, by the gate the shields of the Israelites barred their entrance like a living wall. The group of archers up on the altar became the target of the Babylonians. Hit by arrow or lance, many of the youths fell backwards into the coals of the sacrificial fire. Their own blood smothered the flames. The resistance was broken.

With hue and cry the Chaldeans stormed into the innermost temple, led by their officer Sardapal, with swordsmen clearing the way. The priests had sought shelter within the holy sanctuary. When Sardapal stepped over the threshold, he took a step back before the gleaming gold and the ten burning lamps. A moment later, however, the uncontrolled swordsmen stormed past him, and the slaughter of the unarmed priests followed. The burning lamps toppled over, singeing the clothes of the dead. It grew dark in the defiled room.

Before the curtain to the Holy of Holies the High Priest stood with arms spread open protectively. A soldier sprang at him and ran him through with his sword. The High Priest fell backwards into the Holy of Holies where his blood and his life poured out of him. His voice whispered his last words, "The Ark is saved! Thanks to you, Jeremiah!"

As Sardapal looked about him, it was dead quiet in the room. A last flame flickered restlessly in a lamp as if it were ashamed of giving light to the horrors in the temple. Sardapal gave his soldiers a subdued command, "Keep watch before the door! I will return by the light of day and give directions how to clear the temple. Before that, let no one enter!"

The next morning Sardapal returned with King Nebuchadnezzar's master of the treasury. The dead were removed first. Then the master of the treasury determined what was to be done with the tremendous booty of gold, silver and bronze. He had the golden vessels and instruments set in a pile, and then did the same with the silver and the bronze. He had brought with him the weaponssmiths with their tools. He directed them to break up with their hammers the two enormous metal pillars that stood in front of the temple. They tore the gold plate from the walls in the Holy of Holies, and they beat the two cherubim with their hammers into large lumps of gold. They then hacked into clumps of bronze the enormous bowl of the 'bronze sea' that the twelve bulls had carried aloft. They left a number of the gold and silver vessels untouched. These were singled out to be taken to Babylon to sit in King Nebuchadnezzar's treasure house. Little by little they loaded the temple treasures and metal pieces into wagons and onto camels. A long caravan of plunder brought them to Babylon and into the kingdom of the Chaldeans.

Jeremiah survived the horrors of the destruction of Jerusalem. Still, he also ended up with his hands bound by chains. In the meantime, King Nebuchadnezzar had heard about Jeremiah's prophecy. It pleased him that he had achieved victory as God's envoy of vengeance. He sent the chief of his bodyguards to Jeremiah.

"The king shows you mercy! If it pleases you to come with us and the captured Israelites to Babylon, you are free and will stand under my protection. If, however, you prefer to remain here in this land with the peasants we leave behind, then you may remain here."

Jeremiah answered, "Let me stay behind with my people!" So it happened that Jeremiah did not go to Chaldea as a prisoner. He stayed behind with the peasants and the poor people whom the king left behind, and he comforted them in their desperation.

Daniel

After King Nebuchadnezzar had conquered Jerusalem and brought many prisoners to Babylon, he gave instructions to his steward. "From among the noble families of the Jews, seek out for me several of the best and most able young men. I want them trained to serve in the royal palace. Two aspects are important to me: a handsome figure and a good intelligence! Place them in the palace school together with young men from our land and have them taught in our language like Babylonians. After three years, they should be ready for service and to appear before me."

The steward was very strict in his selection. The young men chosen were Daniel, Hananiah, Mishael and Azariah. They were dressed in beautiful garments and well fed on fatty meats so that their bodies grew strong. They were always given wine to drink, so that they would have a fiery temperament, as was then the belief.

Daniel had a particularly handsome face and noble stature. He said to his three other companions, "Let us stand firmly by one another. We are from the same blood. Drinking wine every day harms our spirit, and the fatty meat from the idol sacrifices will make us dull and fat."

Hananiah answered, "How are we to change anything? We are slaves!"

Daniel responded, "I will speak with the master of the kitchen. He has been kind to me. Lately, he has spoken to me in confidence about his worries."

Straightaway, Daniel went with his three companions to the master of the kitchen. He bowed before him and spoke. "Dear

Master, is there something bothering you? It seems so to me. I would like to do something good for you."

The master of the kitchen was astonished. Indeed, that very morning he had been very annoyed by the chief cook. He responded, "Daniel, what is the good thing you would like to do for me?"

Daniel answered, "I am going to sing for you a song from my homeland." Daniel began to sing in a lively manner, and the other three clapped the beat. The master of the kitchen had never before been so entertained.

"What a fine fellow!" he thought to himself. Then, Daniel even went to him, took his hand, and kissed it.

"Master," he said, "you have it in your power to make the four of us very happy. We come from Judah and have different customs than the Babylonians. May we drink water instead of wine when we eat? May we eat dishes of grain and vegetables instead of rich meats? You see, Master, that is what we were accustomed to in Jerusalem."

The master of the kitchen looked thoughtful. After considering for a while, he answered, "If you should grow thin and bony, the steward will punish me."

Daniel begged, "Master, we would certainly never become bony! Just let us try it out for ten days!"

The master responded, "Good, we can try it out for ten days. But if after five days you begin to look thinner, you must once again eat the rich meats."

After ten days Daniel and his companions looked much better than those who drank wine and ate meat. After that the master of the kitchen did not hesitate to let them eat as they pleased. From time to time he had them cheer him up with a Hebrew song.

In the palace school, the four friends eagerly learned the Chaldean language, geometry and the science of the stars. After three years had passed, all pupils were brought before King Nebuchadnezzar. Among them all, Daniel and his friends stood out for their beauty and knowledge. All four were allowed to enter into the palace service and it went well with them.

Nebuchadnezzar's Dream

Around this time, King Nebuchadnezzar had a dream that disturbed him deeply. He summoned the wise teachers of Babylon and questioned them. "What did I dream this night? Tell me, and interpret what it means."

The wise men responded, "O King, no one can say what another dreams. But when you tell us what you dreamed, we can tell you what it means."

The king grew angry at this evasive answer and said to the captain of the guard, "My wise men are worthless; do away with them!"

Among them was one of Daniel's teachers. Daniel loved this teacher, and when he heard about the king's command, he hastened to the captain and spoke, "Do not slay the wise men! I am their student and tomorrow I will tell the king his dream."

The captain hesitated. Daniel stood so straight and tall before him in his beauty and strength, that finally he responded, "I can wait one day."

Before going to sleep, Daniel soulfully beseeched God to inspire him. And behold, in the night he dreamed the exact same dream that the king had dreamed. Early the next morning Daniel had himself announced at the palace. Immediately he was taken before Nebuchadnezzar.

He began, "The dream that came to you, O King, was of a gigantic statue. Its head was made out of gold, its chest and arms out of silver, its belly out of bronze, its legs out of iron. The feet were made out of iron mixed with clay. Suddenly, a stone broke loose from the mountain. It smote the statue in the feet and crushed them. Then the colossus collapsed upon itself. The stone, however, that destroyed the image, grew to be as high as a mountain and spread itself out over the whole earth."

When Daniel stopped talking, the king stood there looking quite pale; but happily he cried out, "That was it! Yes, that was it!" He gestured that the dream interpreter should come close and stand at his side. He urged him on, "Now, Daniel, tell me what it means!"

Daniel began, "Great power and glory has been bestowed upon you, O King. You are the golden head. After you a lesser kingdom will arise, the silver one. After that a third will arise, a bronze one, which will wage many wars and spread itself wide over the earth. Following that will come an immensely dark reign with rulers of iron who will bring war everywhere. Then a fifth kingdom will arise that will be as mighty as iron but fragile as clay. Its fate is to bring the decline of all. The stone, however, from out of the heights of the celestial mountains, will shatter the earthly kingdom. Then a kingdom of God will grow on the earth that will be eternal and indestructible. God has announced to King Nebuchadnezzar in a dream what will happen in the future."

After hearing these words, the king fell with his face to the ground and was shaken to the very depths of his soul. When he was able to rise again, he spoke to Daniel. "You, noble youth! Your God has inspired you. From now on, be my chief wise man and friend! From this day, you shall be the Master of the Wise Men of Babylon." He showered Daniel with favors and gifts. "Speak a wish, and it will be fulfilled," the king said.

Daniel prayed, "O King, do not punish your wise men, and let my three friends enter in your service together with me as faithful stewards so that we may stay together."

The king was kindly inclined toward Daniel and fulfilled these wishes. From that day on Daniel, Hananiah, Mishael and Azariah were inseparable friends.

The Three Men in the Fiery Oven

King Nebuchadnezzar became ever more powerful and rich. The notion came to the ruler to erect a sign of his power. In the middle of the city, he had his servants set up a golden image that was higher than the houses of Babylon. Then he sent the heralds out with a proclamation: "Every morning when the trumpets resound, the residents of the city are required to throw themselves to the ground and pray to the god of my royal power, which I have erected as a statue. Whoever refuses to do this will be thrown alive into the ovens."

At this time, Daniel was away on a long journey doing the king's business. His three friends, Hananiah, Mishael and Azariah, worked as officials for the king and lived together in one house. Daniel had his own beautiful house with servants, which he had received from the king as a gift.

When they learned of the king's new order, the three friends took council together. "Moses gave to us the commandment forbidding us to serve graven idols. We can not do what the king requires." When the trumpets resounded the next morning, they raised their arms and said, "Great is the Lord, our God!"

Now there were in the king's court other officials who for some time had viewed the three Jewish stewards with envy. They appeared before Nebuchadnezzar and complained. "O King, there are three men in the city who have contempt for your command. They scorn your order to pay homage to your statue. They are Hananiah, Mishael and Azariah!"

A flash of rage flamed up in Nebuchadnezzar. He ordered the three men thrown into the fiery oven as he had threatened. He would come himself and scatter their ashes.

The three men were arrested and the judgment carried out. The king drove to their punishment in a golden chariot. When, however, he looked through an opening into the fiery oven, he saw four men standing upright. The fourth one had an unearthly form. This was an angel that broke the consuming power of the fire.

The king was deeply shocked. He immediately had the door of the oven opened and called out to them, "Hananiah, Mishael, Azariah, come out from there!" Unharmed, they stepped out of the oven; not a hair on their heads had been singed. The king saw the fourth figure floating upwards out of sight. He cried out loud, "Praise be to the God who has saved these men! And I issue this warning: Henceforth whoever speaks ill of the God of the Jews, his house will be turned to rubble!" After this, the king returned the men to their previous office and honor.

Nebuchadnezzar had defeated his enemies among the neighboring peoples and had established a proud and arrogant Babylonian kingdom. Anyone he wished to kill, he could have killed, and likewise, anyone he wished to raise up and honor, he could raise up. He ruled with harshness and contempt of his fellow human beings. That was when a demon took hold of his soul. The king's spirit fell, became beast-like, and he died in madness. His son, Belshazzar, took over the kingship. He was consumed soon by the same overweening arrogance as his father.

Belshazzar's Feast

One night Belshazzar held a great feast in Babylon for the lords of the kingdom. More than a thousand guests were invited. Immense jugs of red wine were passed around and served. The

blood of animals was mixed into the wine, so that before long the young warriors were crying out, shouting and acting crazy. Even the king's concubines joined in; it turned into a bellowing Babylonian drunken orgy. Belshazzar acted worse than all the rest.

As midnight neared, the king summoned the master of the treasury and spoke to him in a drunken voice, "Go get from the treasury the gold and silver goblets and drinking cups that my father pillaged from the temple in Jerusalem!"

When these goblets were brought, which had once been kept sanctified in Solomon's temple, Belshazzar had them filled with blood-stained wine and demanded, "Take the Jewish vessels and drink to the health of our Babylonian gods!" He was the first to grasp a golden goblet; he lifted it high and cried, "Jehovah is dead. Long live Baal!"

Suddenly, all of the lights and lamps began to flicker; many went out. Belshazzar stood there rigidly with the goblet in his hand and stared. His face grew distorted and with a fixed gaze he stared over at the white wall. The hall grew deadly still. A hand appeared out of a cloud and wrote in letters of fire on the wall, *Mene, Mene, Tekel U-Parsin*.

The hand disappeared, but the writing remained. The king grew so frightened that his knees knocked together. He cried out, "Bring me the magicians and the astrologers!" He was not able to take a single step himself; he was not even able to sit down again.

The magi arrived; they pondered and debated this way and that. Not one of them could understand the mysterious words of the writing. Suddenly the king's mother entered the hall. She spoke to Belshazzar. "Once Daniel revealed for your father what was hidden. Have him brought."

Many of the warriors and invited lords slipped away secretly in the dim light. The hall grew ever darker and emptier. Only the gold and silver vessels of the temple shone in the dying light of the torches. The writing on the wall, however, remained luminous. The king fell back into his armchair.

In the meantime, Daniel was fetched with a racing chariot. When he was led into the room, Belshazzar raised his arm and pointed mutely to the writing. Daniel raised his prophetic voice and spoke. "Belshazzar, you have not learned anything from the pitiful way your father died; you have gained no humility. In your arrogance, you have misused the holy vessels of the temple and desecrated them. You have mocked the Lord. Still, you shall know what the spirit hand has written: *Mene* means that your kingdom has come to an end! *Tekel* says that it has been weighed and found wanting. *U-Parsin* means that it will be divided between the Medes and the Persians." Filled with rage, Daniel left the palace.

On that very night, Belshazzar was slain by several of his own soldiers. With his death the writing on the wall vanished.

Very soon after this, the kingdom was conquered by Darius, the king of the Medes. Darius placed Daniel over all the royal officials, since he had heard that a prophetic spirit reigned in him.

From Bel to Babel

In Babylon, the priests built a temple to serve the idol Bel. It was a gigantic image with its mouth wide open. The priests said, "It is necessary in the evening to bring good food into the temple. He consumes great portions of roasted mutton and goats in the course of the night."

It so happened that when the priests had designed the building, they had made a secret entrance to the innermost part of the temple. When the servants of the temple carried in all of the freshly prepared food in large vessels, a large number of people would gather at this show. A priest would then close the temple doors with all sorts of abracadabra. The key would be solemnly delivered over to the safety of the king's steward and on the following morning retrieved from him again. When the empty vessels were carried out the next morning, many people were impressed by the miracle, and they streamed into the temple in order to pray to "the god who eats." As a result, the temple attracted a lot of people. The truth, however, was that the seventy priests retrieved the good food every evening through the secret passageway and enjoyed it with their families. Some even remained in the temple itself and consumed the feast and enjoyed the wine, which had been offered by the jugful to the god Bel.

The king himself did not let a day go by without offering his prayers before Bel. One day, he spoke to Daniel. "Come with me to the temple of Bel. He is a living god; he consumes a large quantity of food."

Daniel responded, "I do not serve idols that have been made by human hands. I pray to the living God, who created heaven and earth."

The king was astonished. "Do you not consider Bel to be a living god? Haven't you seen how much he eats and drinks every night?"

Daniel laughed and said, "High King, do not let yourself be deceived! Bel is made of clay and bronze and has never eaten anything."

Then the king grew angry and summoned the priests. He spoke to them, "If you cannot prove to me that Bel consumes the sacrificial food, then you must die! If you are able to prove it, then Daniel must die!"

Daniel said, "So may it be, O King, as you have spoken."

Then the king went with Daniel and the priests into the temple of Bel. The priests spoke, "Lord, have your servants carry the food within! We will then go outside and let you yourself close the doors. Seal them with your ring. When you return early in the morning and discover that Bel has not consumed everything, then we will gladly die. Otherwise, Daniel should die, for telling lies about us."

At this, the priests left the temple. Once outside, the king had the food placed before Bel on a table. Daniel, however, sent a servant to bring a tub of ashes. As the king watched, he had the ashes scattered over the floor of the temple. Then, they went outside and the king sealed the temple doors with his own ring. During the night, the priests, according to their custom, slipped through the secret passage and devoured everything that was there.

In the gray before the next dawn, the king and Daniel returned to the temple. The seal on the door was untouched. As soon as the door was opened, the king saw the empty table and called out in a loud voice. "Bel, you are a great god!"

Daniel, however, laughed and said, "Behold the floor, my lord, and see the many footsteps from the shoes of the priests."

The king grew furious and had the priests summoned. They were forced to show him the secret passage through which they came and went so they could consume all the food themselves. In anger the king had them slain and gave to Daniel all the power over Bel. He had the idol broken into pieces and the temple of deception destroyed.

Daniel in the Lion's Den

The one hundred twenty royal officials of the palace did not like the honest, faithful Daniel to rule over them. They spoke among themselves, "When it comes to managing the affairs of the state, we cannot find anything bad to say about him. We will have to use his religion, which is not Babylonian, as the means of destroying him."

So the state officials, together with the priests, contrived a plot against Daniel. They wrote a document, which read: "The highest lord in the land is King Darius. In every petition or prayer that is spoken, his name must be mentioned. Whoever disobeys, will be thrown into the lion's den."

The lions were considered in Babylon as the symbol for the royal power. Lions were held in a deep pit, and whenever an enemy of the king's was arrested, he was thrown to the lions to be devoured by them.

The priests and state officials persuaded Darius to sign the edict. Although Daniel was aware of all of this, he continued his practice every day of climbing to the upper floor of his house. There he always opened a window facing west, toward Jerusalem, and prayed to God three times a day in a loud voice.

The priests and officials placed spies to listen. They reported that in all of his prayers, Daniel did not pray to the king. Then they went to Darius and accused him. "Daniel disregards your edict and prays only to his foreign god!" His enemies achieved their end; Daniel was arrested and thrown into the pit with the hungry lions.

But King Darius had a bad feeling in his conscience and spent a particularly restless night. Then he had an intriguing thought: Now it would be revealed if the God of Daniel was truly a living god. If this were the case, He would rescue him in the lion's den.

The next morning, Darius went to the lion's den. He wanted to see with his own eyes how Daniel had fared. When he bent over to look into the pit, behold, there he saw Daniel, alive, and the lions lay at his feet.

The king had him pulled out of the pit with a rope and spoke to him. "Daniel, you are a true servant of the living God. How did He rescue you from the lions?"

Daniel answered, "My God sent an angel to me; he closed the jaws of the lions, so that they could not harm me. Praised be God!"

The king had Daniel's accusers summoned and ordered them thrown into the pit. The lions fell on them and none survived. Darius lifted the restrictions on prayer, and announced that Daniel's God might be worshiped.

Daniel's Prophecy

When Daniel had grown to a worthy old age, God revealed to him the future of human destiny through powerful prophecies and visions. He saw in spirit how in the course of time four beasts would rise out of the sea: the winged lion, a bear-like monster, and the winged panther. The most frightening beast, however, was the fourth that rose out from the abyss. It had giant iron teeth and ten horns, and it destroyed whatever came beneath its feet. In spite of their power, these beasts were defeated by divine beings and their power was taken from them.

On the clouds of the heavens a being rode that was like unto a son of man. The Highest gave him the power to found a kingdom of eternal light. However, before that could come about there would be a time of oppression from the beasts, and human beings would be tested as never before. Then Michael the Archangel would rise up and become the protector and companion-in-arms against the beasts from the abyss.

Daniel wrote all of this down and placed his seal upon the book.

Nehemiah

When the Persian King Cyrus conquered the Babylonian kingdom, the Jew Nehemiah lived at his court serving as a cupbearer. His was a bright spirit and he had a noble bearing, so the king liked to keep him nearby. After the destruction of Jerusalem, Nehemiah had come to Babylon with the long train of prisoners. Now, many years later, he held an important post in the king's court. Frequently he wondered how his brethren were doing in his distant homeland. Was his brother Hanani even alive? How were those who had been left behind?

King Cyrus had allowed the captive Jews from Babylon to return to their homeland and rebuild the temple. Their strength, however, had been broken. Only with great difficulty did the temple walls grow. Often there were long periods of idleness when no one worked. They lacked someone who could inspire them.

King Cyrus' successor was Artaxerxes, and Nehemiah served him as well. Then one day, several foreigners arrived at the entryway to the court. They came from Jerusalem. Nehemiah's brother Hanani was among them. How he looked! His clothing was thin and worn, and he was gaunt as if he had suffered many years of hunger. His eyes shone when his brother, beautifully clothed, embraced him. Then, however, he fell again into sadness. Nehemiah questioned him. "Brother, what can you tell me about Jerusalem?"

"Poor city, poor residents! The city walls are still full of gaps from when we were besieged. The gates are burnt. The ruined entrance offers no protection. The people who live there are often at the mercy of bands of robbers. Jerusalem is a dead city."

Nehemiah had known Jerusalem in its full glory. At this description, he could not withhold his tears. In the night, he could not sleep because he was so full of anguish. He prayed to God. "Is it not possible to bring to an end the bitterness and suffering of Jerusalem?"

The next morning at breakfast, as he filled the royal cup with wine, the king noticed the sadness of his cupbearer. He questioned him, "You look terrible. You have been crying. Are you ill, or is your heart pained?"

Nehemiah had to force himself to hold his tears back as he answered. "O lord, yesterday did I receive news from my brother how badly things stand in my home city of Jerusalem. The city of my ancestors continues to lie in rubble and ruin. Ah, if only I could go there with my brother and rebuild it!"

The king considered a moment and then asked him, "How long would you want to stay there?"

Nehemiah named a length of time, and behold, God had sweetened the king's heart. The king spoke, "If I send you there, you shall be my governor in Jerusalem. Make Jerusalem once again a beautiful city!"

Nehemiah fell to his knees before the king and kissed the hem of his gown. King Artaxerxes gave to him letters to take on his journey in which it was written with the king's seal that Nehemiah was to be the governor of Jerusalem. He had permission to take wood from royal forests for making new gates and for the rebuilding of houses.

Before long, Nehemiah was able to begin the long journey with his brother and their companions. The king sent with him officers and riders for their protection. In this way he would make a dignified entrance into Jerusalem as the king's governor.

A Difficult Rebuilding

When Nehemiah arrived in Jerusalem, he rested from the difficulties of his journey. On the third evening after his arrival he began to inspect the walls of Jerusalem. He made a firm decision in his heart to rebuild the fallen walls. He summoned the priests, the distinguished citizens, and the poor of the city as well. He spoke to them.

"You all know the suffering of our city. The neighboring tribes make fun of you and use force against you, because you are defenseless. By working together, let us once again build the walls of the city and replace the gates. The king of Babylon gives us permission to do as we please. Indeed, he has even promised us wood and beams in order to rebuild the gates. Come, everyone lay a hand to raise the fallen Jerusalem to become a fitting city for the temple! The hand of God is held over my head and brings protection and kindness. God is with us!"

Nehemiah inspired the people with his words. Soon people were busy with cleaning up and working. Nehemiah himself took up pick and shovel in order to give the people a good example. Day after day they worked on the gaps and a new wall was made.

However, before they could mount the first gate, the enemy arrived. The neighboring tribes, the Horonites and the Ammonites, and their leaders wanted to prevent the city from being rebuilt. Frequently, in the evening or in the night, bands came secretly and pulled down what had been built during the day.

From this point on, only half of the people worked at a time, while the others stood watch with lance, bow and arrow, in order to protect their work. Even those who carried the heavy stones always had swords at their sides. Here and there they placed men with trumpets on the wall. When any suspicious band neared, the trumpets blew the alarm, and the enemy was driven away.

They worked from the rose of the dawn until the evening stars appeared. In the night, their work was watched over by armed guards.

Finally the day arrived when all of the holes in the wall were repaired. Only the new gates had not yet been set in place. Nehemiah was always to be found among the workers. Here he hammered or shoveled, there he provided food, and he was always ready to take a turn at the watch. All the people loved him, and his example inspired them with strength and courage.

Then the enemy came up with a new plan. "If we could manage to capture this Nehemiah and do away with him, the people would lose courage, and then we could break their spirit!"

They sent to Nehemiah a deceitful message that he should visit them, so that they could take council together on developing good neighborly relations. Nehemiah realized what their true intentions were and sent word that he had no time at present to leave Jerusalem.

Before long, the strong gates were set into place and it was finally possible to secure a peaceful rest with only a few night watchmen. Nehemiah ordered a great celebration. The priest Ezra read out loud to the people the laws of Moses. They decorated their houses, the gates and the temple with green branches. Everywhere musicians played, people sang songs and took part in dances of joy. They called this the Feast of Booths or *Sukkot*. Through the deeds of Nehemiah, the people who had been tested found new hope and they solemnly promised from this time forward to walk in the ways of the Lord.

Jonah

Jonah was the son of Amittai. When he was a boy he fell seriously ill and was at the point of death. The prophet Elijah gave him back his life. As a result of this experience, a sincere piety arose in the boy's soul. When Jonah grew to be a man, the Lord chose him to be His prophet. It happened in this way.

In the city of Jerusalem there were many people who disregarded the temple and the divine commandments. One night, Jonah heard a voice speaking to him as he awoke from sleep: "Go to Jerusalem! Announce to the people that misfortune will fall upon the city. It will be destroyed!"

Though it was difficult, Jonah made the journey to Jerusalem to deliver this troubling prophecy. At several places in the city and at the entrance to the temple he announced with fiery energy the word of the Lord.

The citizens were shaken. They attended and made amends. They once again followed the commandments and prayed for divine grace and forgiveness. And behold, the Lord softened His anger. Jerusalem was saved from disaster.

From then on, though, Jonah was called a false prophet. He suffered as a result of these words. He decided to travel far away to escape the ridicule of the people. But once more the voice came to him in the night and spoke: "Arise, Jonah, and go to Nineveh, that great city of the Assyrians, and pronounce to them their destruction, for their misdeeds cry to Heaven!"

At this command, Jonah felt great distress and doubt: Would the same thing happen to him as in Jerusalem? If the people of Nineveh also change their ways after the prophecy, the city will not be destroyed. Once again they will cry: There goes the false prophet!

Jonah thought how he might avoid the divine command. He fled to the port city of Joppa and thought he would board a ship and sail to the ends of the earth. He found a sailing ship at anchor and asked the ship's captain, "Will you take me with you?"

The ship was just getting ready to sail to distant Tarshish. So the answer he received was, "We're sailing very far away, almost to the ends of the earth." Jonah paid immediately for passage, and they took him with them.

There were passengers from different peoples and lands on the ship. They had hardly traveled for a day over the water when a terrible storm blew up. The travelers called to their gods and begged for their lives. Jonah, however, had crawled deep into the hold of the ship and had fallen into a deep sleep. In his distress, the ship's captain came to him, shook him until he woke up and cried out to him, "We are all on deck terrified for our lives, and you are sound asleep! You are a Hebrew! Your God is supposed to be powerful. Get up and call out to him to save us!"

But Jonah had just had a very strange dream. He answered the captain, "Throw me into the sea and the water will grow still once again!"

The captain was astonished at his talk and relayed it to the others. They thought that the storm had confused Jonah's mind, and they did not want to do that to him. They threw goods and supplies into the sea as they tried to make the ship lighter. They steered toward the coast, but the storm, wind and waves drove the ship again out into the wild sea. The wooden ribs of the ship cracked at their joints. The sailors were giving up. Then Jonah came again to them and called out, "This storm arose because of me, because

I have disregarded the word of the Lord. Throw me into the sea, and the storm will pass!"

They took hold of Jonah and thrust his feet into the water. The blowing of the wind let up somewhat. When they pulled him out again, the wind grew stronger, and an immense fish appeared. The waves were threatening to swallow the ship. Finally, they gave Jonah over to the torrential waters. The storm passed.

The immense fish swallowed Jonah whole. He lay in the body of the fish as in a coffin. He lost his senses, but he did not lose his life. Pictures passed before Jonah's inner eye like in an immense dream. He saw what the Earth was like at the beginning of Creation. He gazed upon the light of Paradise and Noah's Ark. He saw Moses and the people of Israel crossing the Red Sea. He looked upon the higher world with its Heavenly Hosts as well as into the underworld with its dark demons. Then, however, there arose the light of the temple of God and he was allowed to enter with the initiates and pray with them. He spoke these words in his prayer:

Lord, where can I flee? You are everywhere.
If I were to take the wings of the rosy dawn and go dwell at
the ends of the ocean, there You would also be! O Lord,
I wish to serve You and fulfill Your will!

Then the fish swam toward the coast. It had carried Jonah for three days in its body, and it spat him out onto the land. Jonah now began the long journey to the city of Nineveh. He wanted to proclaim there, as the Lord had commanded him, the city's destruction. He did this now with a willing heart.

Nineveh was an immense royal city. In the market places and in front of the temples, Jonah lifted up his powerful prophetic voice. The people listened to him and bemoaned, "Oh, terrible! Poor us! In forty days calamity will befall us, all because of our sins!"

The king had Jonah brought before him, and Jonah spoke severely with him. The king was deeply affected. He tore his gown and strewed ashes over his head in mourning. Immediately he had it proclaimed in the city: "Every citizen will fast for three days. Leave off your evil ways and turn to good deeds. Pray to the Lord God that He have pity upon us!"

Since all the people had been struck by great fear, they followed the king's orders strictly and begged God for mercy. And the Lord let go of His anger and did no harm to the city.

When the forty days had passed, Jonah feared that once again the people would think he was a false prophet. This grieved him greatly. In the following night he had a strange dream: He lay in the burning sun. A leafy tree grew tall beside him and gave him cooling shade. A gigantic worm crawled by and attacked the tree so that the leaves dried out. The heat of the sun burned down on Jonah. He grew so miserable that he thought he would prefer to die. Suddenly, the voice of the night spoke to him: "Behold, Jonah, you have pity on a dried-out tree. How much more might I have pity upon a destroyed city and its many people! Let us rejoice over the repentance of its citizens!"

When Jonah awoke, he bowed his face down to the earth. He was ashamed of himself that for a moment he had let his indignation get the upper hand. How much better it was to be considered a false prophet than for the city to be destroyed. And he praised the divine mercy.

Heliodorus

When Jerusalem had lived for a long period of time in peace, the temple began to receive many rich gifts. If someone in Palestine had come to a wealth of gold and silver, or had with great effort put away savings, they trusted their belongings to the priests in the temple for safekeeping. It was there that they could be stored most securely. In this way, great treasures were heaped up in the temple's side chambers.

The High Priest Onias guarded these possessions, which were in his trust. They were to remain in the protection of the temple until the owner had need of them and asked for their return.

The rumor of riches lying in the temple made its way to the ears of the Assyrian king. One day he spoke to Heliodorus, his captain at the court. "My supply of gold and silver has grown low from my last campaign. Go, in my name, to Jerusalem. Take with you a troop of soldiers. The city owes me fealty. Demand that the priests show to you the treasure in the temple. Leave a small part of what you find in the temple; take the rest and return here to add it to my own treasure house. The priests will not dare to refuse my command."

When Heliodorus arrived in Jerusalem, he was warmly received by the High Priest Onias as the emissary of the king. However, when Heliodorus told him what he had been sent to do, Onias was deeply shocked. He tried to explain the situation. "Look, Heliodorus, the greater part of the treasure in the temple has been entrusted to us on loan from many of our citizens. If you take this away, then many hundred people will have been deceived."

Heliodorus replied, "Take me to the treasure rooms! In the name of the king, I must see the treasure with my own eyes."

Once again, the High Priest Onias, together with the other priests, tried to persuade Heliodorus not to do this. The terrible news had already leaked out of the temple and a great cry of protest arose in the city. The priests formed a ring around the fire altar and cried to God, entreating for help. But neither talk, lament, nor prayer helped. Heliodorus forced them to bring him to the treasure chambers. The High Priest Onias, disheartened and pale from the shock, was accompanied by stern-faced soldiers.

While Heliodorus and his soldiers were following the High Priest to the treasure, they were overcome by the appearance of a powerful, divine sign. Heliodorus and his band were suddenly flooded by an otherworldly light. The air was filled with a thunder like the trampling of wild horses. Heliodorus watched as a luminous horse with a frightening rider in golden armor came riding down upon him. The horse threw him to the ground with his front hooves. The horse and rider dashed on, followed by two powerful looking figures who struck Heliodorus with the flat of their swords. He fell unconscious and lay there as still as death.

His soldiers had seen the lightning flash and heard the thunder but had seen nothing of either horse or shining companions. When all the commotion was over, they saw Heliodorus lying as if dead on the stone floor. In shock and trembling, they lifted him and carried him away. The priests praised God's omnipotence. When news of what had happened in the temple reached the city, the people rejoiced. There was singing and dancing in every lane.

Not long after this, three soldiers hastened back to the temple. They beseeched the High Priest Onias. "Save our captain's life! He has still not come to his senses. He is drawing his last breath!"

Onias considered his choices. If Heliodorus died, the king would think that they had murdered him. If he recovered, then Heliodorus would be able to bear witness to the omnipotence of God. With this in mind, he made a sacrifice of entreaty that Heliodorus would grow healthy once again, and he prayed out of a deep reverence.

In the chamber where Heliodorus lay, his consciousness slowly returned to him. To his left and to his right he saw two divine youths. One of them spoke to him, "Give thanks to the High Priest Onias! For his sake, the Lord has given you back your life. Wherever you go, proclaim His divine power!" Following these words, the two figures disappeared.

Heliodorus was healed. He went to Onias and thanked him for the gift of his life, and he made sacrifice to the Lord God. When he was well, he journeyed back to his king. Wherever he went, he told about the might of the Lord that had been revealed to him in the temple in Jerusalem. The king wanted to know if he meant by this that he should send someone else to the treasure chamber. Heliodorus responded, "Do such a thing only to your worst enemy, for God is powerful in that place!"

Job

There was a man in the land of Uz whose name was Job. It was not difficult for him, day by day, to walk the path of righteousness and to avoid evil. Seven sons and three daughters were born to him. He was rich with land and herds of cattle and camels, and his children lived in peace with one another. He lacked nothing of earthly good fortune. Every day Job thanked the Lord for all the gifts in his life.

It so happened that the Hosts of Heaven came before God in order to hold a heavenly council. Approaching from below, out of the darkness, came Satan. He also wanted to be present. The angels looked to God, but He let Satan approach. So the angels were not able to prevent it from happening.

In this world of light, Satan appeared like a dark fleck. The Lord addressed him and asked, "Where are you coming from? What do you have to tell me?"

Satan answered, "I have been wandering on the earth, and I have noticed that always more and more people follow the voices of my demons."

The Lord asked, "Have you not noticed Job, my faithful servant? There is no one like him in all the lands. He is filled with kindness and piety. Evil does not touch him. He gives no heed to your demons."

Satan responded, "It is not for nothing that Job is faithful in Your service. You have bestowed upon him every kind of earthly good fortune possible. Only stretch out Your hand and lay it heavily upon everything that he has. Bring him misfortune, and he will also curse You. That is the way with human beings!"

The Lord spoke, "Well, then, everything of earthly value that Job possesses is given into your hands. His soul, however, you may not touch!"

Satan replied, "So may it be! I will do a good job of it! I will pile on his head misfortune upon misfortune, until his mouth denies You in the midst of his despair!"

With these words, Satan went away in triumph. The Lord took council with the Heavenly Hosts concerning the fate of humanity.

The Test

One day, while Job was in prayer, he said, "Hear, O Lord, the voice of your servant, Job! How can we live righteously before Your eyes, all-powerful God?

You shake the earth, so that the pillars tremble.
You cause the sun to rise and set.
You spread the heavens like a carpet
And move the ocean in its ebb and flow.
You created the stars of the Great Bear in the heavens,
Bright Orion and all the sparkling lights.
Your brilliance, Your goodness, O Most Mighty,
Shines over my head.
You cause me to wander in a good house,
And Your grace endures forever.

Hardly had Job ended his prayer, when a messenger burst into his house. He stood before Job and spoke, "O lord, forgive me, that I disturb the peace of your house!"

Job did not even have a chance to greet this messenger before he hurried further to report. "The most terrible thing has happened in your fields! Your servants were plowing with the oxen and your donkeys were grazing nearby. Suddenly, thieves from Saba fell upon them and hustled the animals away. They struck down your servants with the edges of their swords. I was the only one to escape to come and tell you of this misfortune."

With these last words, a second messenger burst into the house. When he had caught his breath, he spoke to Job, "Forgive me, O lord, that I disturb the peace of your house! I was with your shepherds out in the fields with the sheep. Suddenly, an immense, fiery lightning bolt fell out of heaven, right into our midst, and struck down sheep and servants. Only I escaped to come and tell you."

In that moment, they could hear the steps of still a third messenger. When he had caught his breath, he reported, "O lord, forgive me that I disturb the peace of your house. This morning, as is our custom, we brought your camels to drink. We were overrun by three bands of Chaldeans who drove all the animals before them. The keepers were all cut down with the sword. I alone escaped to come and report this misfortune to you."

When he had finished speaking, a fourth messenger approached with a heavy step. He hardly dared to open his mouth to speak. Obviously shaken, he attempted. "O lord, how should I stand before you? I have come to report a tragic misfortune. Your sons and daughters were eating and drinking in their eldest brother's house, the first born. Suddenly from the desert a powerful storm wind blew up. It was so strong that it knocked the house down onto the heads of all the young people inside and they were crushed to death. I alone survived to come and tell you of this." After reporting this terrible event, the messenger sank to his knees and covered his face.

Job jumped up and in his pain tore his garments. Then he fell to the ground. When he once again came to his senses, he prayed with these words:

Naked I came into the world; naked will I again depart!
O, my eyes, what you have gazed upon is washed away!
O, my heart, what you have loved is wiped away!
The Lord has given,
And the Lord has taken.
Praised be the name of the Lord!

Satan had been quietly listening to all that occurred in Job's house and was waiting for the moment when he would curse everything. Job, however, despite the great pain over his loses, remained humble and faithful.

Then the voice of the Lord pressed upon Satan: "Behold! In such pain, and still Job does not stray from his piety."

Satan responded, "Everything that a human being has will be gladly given up for the sake of his earthly life! Lay a heavy hand upon Job's body, upon his flesh and bones, bring upon him illness and pestilence! Then he will curse You to Your face."

"Let it be, then," said the Lord. "Test him! He is in your power; only spare his life!"

Satan inflicted terrible sores all over Job's body, from head to foot. While he lay sick and in pain, his wife approached him and spoke, "Job, misery upon misery has the Lord brought upon you. He now tortures your body with illness. Do you still hold true to Him? Curse your God and die!"

Job answered, "You speak foolishness! You have received so much good from God! Why should we not also accept this test in our misfortune?"

Indignant, his wife left him. Once again alone, all his misery lay heavily upon Job. He called out in the darkness of his chamber, "Why did my mother give birth to me? Why did I not die lying on my mother's breast? The hand of fate has been laid heavily upon me and has broken me through and through!"

In the night, Job perceived a voice in the darkness that whispered, "Job, deny your God! Curse His name! He has tossed you, His faithful servant, like a worm into the dust!"

Job recognized the tempter's voice as Satan. He responded into the darkness, "Even if the heavens crack above me and the earth opens up the abyss beneath me, this I know, that a Redeemer lives and will one day awaken me to new life!"

As these words echoed, Job heard something like a rumbling, a tumult and an outcry. Satan had been overcome and he plunged into the abyss.

From this day forward Job began to heal. All of his brothers, sisters and friends gathered around him. They comforted him in his misfortune and gave him gifts of sheep, cattle and silver. The years passed. He once again had sons, daughters and grandchildren. Grateful, he lived a long life, well over one hundred years.

Among themselves the angels in Heaven said, "When a man as plagued as Job is still able to make himself so strong against Satan, by how much more must we, the angels in Heaven, also do the same!"

Judas Maccabeus

The powerful King Antiochus of Assyria was successful in conquering the Pharaoh's kingdom of Egypt. Unfortunately, the little land of Israel was squeezed between the two great kingdoms of Assyria and Egypt. On his return home, following his great victory, Antiochus marched with his army through Palestine and came to Jerusalem. He plundered the temple, robbed all the treasures and had the gold leaf torn off the temple walls. He destroyed the temple walls and had many Jews put to the sword. Throughout Jerusalem a great outcry and much profound suffering was heard.

Antiochus had a solid Assyrian fortress built in Jerusalem. From then on, his soldiers ruled the city and the people with a heavy hand. Many residents fled into the mountains. Antiochus released a proclamation that only his own idol worship was permitted throughout the kingdom. He stationed enough armed guards to insure that this order would be followed. At this, even more people fled from Jerusalem into the mountains. They sought refuge in caves in their attempt to avoid this tyranny.

In the middle of the city, on the place where the temple lay in ruins, Antiochus had a large idol set up with an altar. He required that it would be honored with sacrifices. He forced the Jews to burn all their holy books and parchments. In any house, where such books were still found, the people who lived there were killed.

At this time, there lived a priest by the name of Mattathias. He had five sons and lived in the mountain city Modin. Mattathias complained, "O misery, that I was born to see the misfortune of my people and the destruction of the holy city! My hands are tied and my feet are bound! My mouth grows dumb through the might of the Assyrians. I sit still and watch as the holy city is destroyed!"

The strong sons of Mattathias spoke. "Father, whatever else might happen, we hold with you the faith in the one God of our people!"

It was not long before an envoy from King Antiochus came to the city of Modin. He had his soldiers erect an idol with an altar in the middle of the city. He summoned the priest Mattathias to him and said, "You are the most influential and highest priest of this city. You have many sons and are held in high regard. Before all the people you are to bring an offering of incense to the god. The king will be kindly inclined toward you and will send you wealth and honor."

When the envoy had finished speaking, a Jew whom the king had bribed approached the altar in order to light the sacrificial fire. Mattathias was overtaken by a violent rage. And since he was a large man, like lightning he tore the sword from one of the guards and stabbed him. In one bound he leapt upon the man making the fire and killed him on the altar. His five sons forcefully overturned the stone altar.

With a loud voice Mattathias called out to the people standing around, "Whoever holds to the covenant with the Lord, our God, join me! We will leave this city!" The soldiers of the envoy stared in shock and fled immediately.

Mattathias left Modin with his sons and many faithful followers. They fled into the mountains. Father Mattathias knew that he did not have the strength and enough life left in him to wage a long battle against the Assyrians. He spoke with his sons. "Simon, listen! From all my sons, you are the wisest. Your brothers should follow your counsel!"

To Judas Maccabeus he said, "You are strong and a hero! You are to be the leader and protect your people against the raging heathens!" Then Mattathias was overcome by grief. He blessed his sons and died.

From all over the land the sons of Israel and Judah were drawn to join Judas Maccabeus. They armed themselves and began making war against the tyrannical invaders. Wherever they went, they overturned the altars of the foreign idols and battled bravely against the heathen. Judas Maccabeus wielded his sword with the courage of a lion. Simon offered prudent counsel. The Maccabee brothers were always in the forefront and pressed the enemy to retreat. The strength of the Lord was with them. Their boldness caused great fear among the Assyrians.

When King Antiochus heard about all these events, his rage grew great. He collected a large army and gave orders to his general Lysiam. "March against the Israelites! Exterminate this rebellious people!" With battle elephants, cavalry and countless foot soldiers, they marched against Palestine.

When Judas Maccabeus gazed from his lookout upon the enemy force that was marching against him, he prayed to God. "Praise be to You, Lord, who by David's hand slew the giant Goliath. We pray to You, do not let us, in this righteous battle, fall in defeat!"

Following this prayer, they attacked the enemy from the heights. By throwing stones, the Israelites were able to panic the horses and elephants. This caused such confusion among the Assyrians that before the battle had even begun, many were already fleeing the field. Judas Maccabeus and the Israelites were victorious.

Judas and his brothers took counsel together. "Let us now march to Jerusalem and rebuild the destroyed sanctuary!"

They did what they intended. They destroyed the idols that had been erected; they cleansed and purified the sanctuary and rebuilt the temple. They had new vessels and lamps cast from the gold and silver plundered from the Assyrian camp. When they were ready once again to kindle the holy fire on the altar in front of the temple, the Israelites who had fled the city returned from the desert and caves and mountains. For the length of six days, they celebrated joyfully and made many offerings of thanks.

King Antiochus received word from his messengers about the destruction of his army. He was so horrified that the threads of his life were torn asunder, and he died like a moth that flies into the flame.

Judas Maccabeus and his brothers still had to ward off the attacks of heathen bands that lived on their borders, but in Jerusalem the fire on the altar before the temple burned day and night once again.

The Alliance with Rome

Judas Maccabeus lent his ear to the talk of Roman merchants. "Far across the sea Rome has become the largest empire of the earth. The Roman armies on land are immense, just as their ships are numerous upon the water. Rome has conquered both smaller and larger kingdoms and taken them under its protection. However, they do not tell any people what gods they should pray to. The ruler in Rome permits each people to follow its own beliefs and protects them from foreign attack."

As a result of this talk, Judas Maccabeus thought: Would not Rome's power be good protection for us Israelites? Then the Assyrians would have to leave us in peace!

He chose two of his friends who were knowledgeable in the ways of the world, John and Jason. He sent them as ambassadors over the sea to Rome. They were to arrange with the Romans an alliance based upon friendship.

The Romans were very open to any nation that would come and ask for protection. They had the conditions of the alliance written on a metal tablet. They sent a representative of the empire with servants and guards to Jerusalem in order to confirm the friendship between the two nations. Rome had already defeated the Assyrians in war. The Israelites could live for a long time in peace, now that they stood under Rome's protection. This is how it came about that in Jerusalem, when the Messiah Jesus Christ appeared, the Roman Pontius Pilate represented the Roman empire as governor.

From this time on Judas Maccabeus and his brothers were held in honor in the people's memories. They had saved Israel from the powerful Assyrians and from complete destruction. They had brought peace to their land after hard-fought battles and prepared the way for the appearance of the Messiah.

John the Baptist

In the days of Herod, King of the Jews, there lived a priest by the name of Zechariah. His wife, Elizabeth, was very unhappy. She was growing older and had not been blessed with a child. This caused her a great deal of distress. Then something unusual happened.

Her husband, Zechariah, was chosen by lot, as was the custom among the priests, to make the burnt offering in the temple for one day. Outside, the crowd waited in prayer for his blessing. When Zechariah began his sacrifice in the temple sanctuary, a light appeared next to the altar. An angel spoke, "Zechariah, your prayer has been heard. Your wife will give birth to a son. His name shall be John. He will be filled with the Holy Spirit and with the strength of the prophet Elijah. He will prepare for the Lord the way for blessing all of humanity. Rejoice!"

Zechariah was deeply astonished. He asked, "How is this possible? For I am old and my wife is past her prime."

The angel answered, "I am Gabriel, sent by God, to bring these glad tidings to you. And you will remain silent about these things until the day your son is born, so that all doubt may pass from you about the miraculous ways of God."

The angel disappeared. Outside, the people were waiting impatiently for Zechariah to return to bestow upon them the blessing of the sacrifice. When he finally emerged from the temple, he had lost his voice. Without a word, he made signs in the air with his hands and in this way blessed them silently. The men and women there were perplexed and asked one another, "What happened to Zechariah in the temple that took his speech away? Was there an appearance?"

When after several days he still could not speak, these events were talked about throughout the land.

The Strange Encounter

When Elizabeth was in the sixth month of her pregnancy with her child John, the angel Gabriel appeared also to Mary of Nazareth. He announced to her an auspicious birth. Not long after this, an inner voice spoke to her: "Go to Elizabeth and Zechariah! Stay with them until the birth of their child."

Mary then traveled into the hill country of Judah to the city where her kinswoman and husband lived. She entered their house, greeted Elizabeth with a clear voice and embraced her. The child in Elizabeth's body jumped for joy. Elizabeth became filled with the Holy Spirit and these words poured out of her: "Blessed be you, Mary, and the child that you will bring to the light of day! When the sound of your greeting reached my ears, the child in my body leapt for joy."

Mary stayed with Elizabeth for three months. The two of them were filled with the warmth of joyful expectation and love. Frequently they spoke with one another. "What will our two children bring to the world? They have both been sent to the earth, and the Archangel Gabriel has announced their coming."

When three more months had passed, Elizabeth gave birth to John, and Mary returned home. Six months later in Bethlehem, Mary gave birth to her child, who was to become the Messiah.

John with the Essenes

When John had grown to be a young man, he was compelled by an inner restlessness to go out into the world. One day when he was tending sheep in the field, an old man in a long white gown approached him. The stranger came and sat beside him. John offered him water to drink from his leather flask.

With thanks, the old man quenched his thirst. He began to speak with John. He gazed deeply into the young man's soul and said, "You are not appointed to watch over sheep all your life. Behold, I belong to the brotherhood of the Essenes on the Dead Sea."

John asked, "To what do you aspire as a community?"

The Essene answered, "In the souls of human beings, evil and wickedness have their way. Hate, lies, mistrust, discord and illnesses have taken over. If human beings continue to live in this darkness of the soul, they will perish."

John asked, "Can they not be helped?"

The Essene answered, "Every human being must begin with himself. And in order for him to do this with his whole soul, we have for a long time now been establishing communities. Through wakefulness and daily practice, we learn how to strengthen the good person within us, so that we learn to control evil and keep it far away from us. This strengthens the spirit. Many of us are able to heal illnesses and to lead people on a better path."

"How does one become an Essene?"

The stranger answered, "We accept young people your age to join us. We instruct them in writings rich in wisdom. We show them how the spirit can grow and the soul find peace through moderation and a pure life."

As the Essene spoke, a mild brightness streamed from his eyes. John was suddenly moved in his heart and asked, "Could I also become an Essene? My father, Zechariah, is dead. I am free to go my own way."

The Essene answered, "Think it over well, young fellow! You still have a mother! If you still think the same way after seven days, then look for us in Qumran. The brothers will take counsel together to decide if they will accept you for a trial period. I am Brother Hiskia. Ask for me! Discuss this ahead of time with your mother and relatives. After all, if you should join us, it is best to come accompanied by good wishes!"

After speaking these words, the Essene made a sign on John's forehead. John kissed his two hands in thankfulness and watched as the white figure disappeared toward the east among the palm trees.

On the Dead Sea

A full week passed. John traveled to the Essene settlement near the Dead Sea. The simple stone walls sat silently in the evening light. It was so still that he nearly did not dare to knock at the gate. He sat down on a stone step. When he finally found the courage to tap with his shepherd's staff, it took a good long while until the wooden bar was pushed back and the gate opened.

"What is it you desire?" asked the man who stepped out.

The youth answered, "Brother Hiskia told me to ask for him here."

"Come in! What is your name?"

"John, the son of Zechariah."

At that moment, they heard the sound of a gong. The Essene spoke, "Come in! The brothers are gathering for evening devotions. Go stand over there at the wall. Hiskia will also be there."

John watched as numerous figures dressed in white stepped in silently. Each one of them had placed his right arm over his breast. They formed a circle and began a humming sort of song. Now the brothers placed their hands on one another's shoulders and the circle began to turn. The humming gave way to a prayer. The circle once again stood still; all of them bent down to the ground on their knees. Eyes and arms were directed upwards toward the night sky as they prayed to the stars. Then they all together stood up again, and the brothers disappeared to their cells.

Hiskia had noticed John's arrival. He approached him and greeted him in a fatherly manner. He showed him where he could spend the night on dry sand in the courtyard. From a clay jug he poured water into a cup and handed it to the youth, adding two figs to it. "Here is your evening meal. Tomorrow I will introduce you to the brothers. When we are called in the morning to rise, you may join us in the courtyard for our prayers to the sun. Have a blessed rest!"

In this way John joined the community of the Essenes. He stayed with them for many years. He learned the wisdom of the brotherhood from ancient parchment scrolls. He learned the art of speaking. He exercised humility through renouncing the pleasures of the world, as a true Essene. One wish, however, grew ever stronger within him: He wished to go out to be among his people. On those occasions when he did go out, he was oppressed by the many ways the darkness had taken over through lies, hate, quarrels, godlessness and the many forms of misfortune and illness. Repeatedly, he visited villages and the huts of the poor to bring light into the darkness and into the suffering of the people.

The Preacher in the Desert

After living with them for many years, John loosened his ties with the Essene community. The call had come to him to go and wait at the waters of the Jordan for those people who wanted to hear what he had to say. John built for himself a simple hut, which protected him from the rain and the burning sun. It was the custom among the Essenes that when someone was ready to purify himself of his sins through repentance, they would dip him in the water. Many people sought out John on the Jordan to hear his sermons. His words were powerful and gave people courage and new strength for their lives.

John said, "Darkness has descended upon our world. Evil has taken over. Dull eyes can no longer see the wonders of the work of creation. Ears can no longer hear rightly when the divine word is spoken. It no longer reaches the hearts of the people; they are hardened like stone. They chase after earthly pleasures. Their spirit, their souls have grown pale. In this way the Adversary can attack them from within. The human race is falling to ruin through its sins.

"Change your souls, O people. Recognize the darkness you live in! Awaken to the light of the world!" More and more people began traveling to the river Jordan to hear John speak. Following every sermon many of them desired to be baptized by him and resolved to lead better lives.

The priests and Pharisees of the temple in Jerusalem were growing envious of John, since he was attracting so many people. Several of them decided to go to the Jordan themselves and hear what this strange prophet had to say. They thought, "He will say things that will give us the chance to attack him and force him to be silent. The temple is the middle of the world, not the Jordan!"

They went and mingled into the crowd, somewhat off to the side. First, the prophet spoke about the light that shines into the darkness but is not seen. Suddenly, however, he turned to the priests and the Pharisees and spoke directly to them. "Your wisdom has grown dull. You are possessed by the desire to control. You have become a brood of serpents!"

In rage, the priests and Pharisees stomped away. From this time onward, their enmity toward the prophet of the Jordan grew. They spread the rumor that John was stirring the people up against King Herod. At the same time, a number of people came to John and asked him, "Are you the Messiah, the one who has been promised to us?"

John answered, 'I am not the One. I prepare the way for Him. He will come after me. I am not worthy to loosen His sandals. I baptize you with water. He, on the other hand, will baptize you with the fire of the Holy Spirit!"

A small band of disciples had formed around John, and he instructed them on the inner paths of the soul. When so many people came to the river, these disciples were also allowed to perform the baptisms. Before long, there were thousands who had been baptized and were awaiting the coming of the Messiah.

The Baptism of Jesus

John received from within the message that the Messiah was coming down to the Jordan. He saw Jesus of Nazareth coming from a distance, alone, a man bathed in light. Above him, however, lay a shadow of pain, from the suffering and misery of humanity. John went to meet him and wanted to bow down at his feet. Jesus, however, ordered him, "John, baptize me!"

John's disciples stepped aside. Two of them held the robes of Jesus.

When Jesus stepped into the river, John scooped up water with his baptism bowl and let it pour out in three streams: over the back of his head, in the middle, and over his forehead and face. He spoke as he let the water stream forth. "May the Lord God pour His blessings over you, through the Cherubim and Seraphim, in wisdom, love and strength!"

There sounded a great tumult from above. Thunder echoed and the heavens opened up. In a glowing cloud, a white-winged figure descended, like a dove, that showered Jesus with a stream of light. Out of the thunder the voice of God sounded, "This is My beloved Son!"

John was overcome at the sight of the Heavenly Hosts, and he knew: Now is the *Christ* among human beings as the Son of God. When he gazed up the Jordan, he saw a dark cloud, all balled up, filled with black figures led by the princes of Hell. He knew then that all of the forces of Hell would stand against the work of the Messiah on earth.

When Jesus the Christ withdrew from that place, John spoke to the two disciples who had stood by him: "Behold Him! Along the banks of the river goes the greatest Man of God, humble like a lamb! My work is completed. He will grow, and I must wane. Go follow Him and receive His words!"

Concerning the Death of the Baptist

The Pharisees and the priests never forgave John for calling them a brood of serpents. They sought protection from King Herod, the son of the king who had murdered the children of Bethlehem. The priests gave him rich gifts from the temple treasures so that he would do their will. Herod accused John the Baptist of misleading and inciting the people. He had his soldiers arrest him and throw him into prison at the fortress of Macharus.

Two of John's disciples became followers of Christ and experienced His miracles. They were able to go and visit John in prison. They told him about the deeds of Christ. "He gives sight to the blind, the lame walk again, lepers are healed, the deaf hear again, the dead are risen up!"

Great joy arose in John, and he said, "I was allowed to spread the light of the moon. He is the splendor of the sun!"

When the news was brought to Christ and the disciples that Herod had ordered John killed, he said, "Since Adam, there has lived no purer soul in human form. He is the angel who prepared the way as the last prophet. Truly, he is Elijah! Comfort yourselves! From now on he will be in our midst!"

Made in the USA
Middletown, DE
18 June 2023